# HOUSEHOLD FIRST

## for Physical Therapy Practice Owners

**Run Your Household Like a Business — Build a Practice that Serves Your Life**

*By*

Eric S. Miller

Written By Eric S. Miller



ISBN: 978-1-937205-32-4
Published by Sage Assets, LLC, Florida, USA

For more information contact:
Econologics Financial Advisors, LLC
2401 West Bay Drive, Suite 603
Largo, FL 33770
info@econologics.com
www.HouseholdFirst.com

# Acknowledgments

Probably the only real regret I have is waiting until I was 45 to get married and have a family. While it can sometimes feel combustible and chaotic, the prodigious amount of affection and love I have for my family cannot be overstated. The serenity and enjoyment they bring into my life place them first on the list of those to whom I give thanks.

To my clients, and to the other healthcare practice owners and professionals I have I've had the privilege to work with—this book is dedicated to you. Your challenges, questions, and real-world experiences have shaped the ideas in these pages. You've allowed me to see firsthand what works, what doesn't, and what truly matters when it comes to building a life—not just a business practice.

To my business partner and the team at Econologics Financial Advisors—you are the ballast on the ship. You provide stability and control, and I want to thank you for your commitment to our mission. The work you do every day helps change the financial lives of our clients and brings the "Household First" philosophy to life.

To my colleagues in the healthcare industries EFA serves and to those dedicated to improving the field as a whole—thank you for your input, guidance, and conversations. You've helped shape our perspective and reinforce the importance of making sure those who care for others also take care of themselves financially.

And finally, thanks to you—the reader. By reading this book, you are investing your time to better your future. My hope is that it helps you think differently, act intentionally, and ultimately build a practice that serves your life.

# TABLE OF CONTENTS

# INTRODUCTION

You are one of the most educated professionals in your field. You spent years in school, took on significant debt, and came out the other side with the skills to build something real. And you did. You built a practice that serves your community, employs a team, and generates the kind of income most people only read about.

So why does your financial life still feel like it is one bad month away from chaos?

Why does retirement feel like a moving target? Why do you have a financial advisor but still feel like something is missing? Why does the practice keep growing while the household stays stuck?

You are not bad with money. You are not lazy or irresponsible. You are highly intelligent and you work harder than almost anyone you know.

The problem is that nobody ever showed you how the two most important financial entities in your life — your practice and your household — are supposed to work together. You were trained to be an exceptional clinician. You figured out the business side mostly on your own.

And the household? It got whatever was left over.

That is what this book is about. Not working harder. Not finding a new investment. Not maxing out one more retirement account. It is about finally putting the right structure in place so that everything you have already built starts working the way it was always supposed to.

Your practice exists to serve your life. This book shows you how to make that a reality.

***It is possible to win in your practice and lose in your life at the same time.***

### *The Problem No One Is Talking About*

Physical Therapy practice owners are among the most educated, hardworking, and service-driven professionals in the country. You spent years in school, took on significant debt, sacrificed time and energy that most people will never understand, and built something that genuinely serves your community. You did not do it for the money. But you deserve the financial rewards that come with it.

The reality for far too many owners is something different. High income, but a surprisingly low net worth. A practice that grows while the household stays financially stuck. Retirement accounts that exist but never feel like enough. A creeping sense that the practice is consuming your life rather than funding it.

The reason is not a lack of intelligence or effort. It is a structural problem. Most physical therapy practice owners have been taught to run their business with precision and intention, and to manage their household finances as an afterthought. The practice has a strategy. The household runs on hope.

This book is about fixing that. Not someday. Now.

### *Why This Book Exists*

Econologics Financial Advisors was built specifically to serve healthcare practice owners. Over the course of thousands of hours working directly with physical therapists, dentists, physical therapists, and other private practice owners across the country, one pattern emerged more consistently than any other: the financial disconnect between a thriving practice and a struggling household.

We have sat across from owners with millions in annual revenue who could not answer basic questions about their household finances. We have watched brilliant clinicians make avoidable financial mistakes simply because no one ever showed them a better framework. And we have had the privilege of watching those same owners, once given the right tools and the right guidance, transform not just their financial situation but their relationship with their practice entirely.

This book was not written from an ivory tower or assembled from generic financial advice. It was distilled from real conversations, real cases, and real outcomes with real physical therapy practice owners. Every concept in these pages has been tested against the actual challenges you face.

### *The Household First Framework*

The central idea of this book is simple but often counterintuitive: your household is not a byproduct of your practice. It is the point of your practice.

Your practice exists to serve your life, not the other way around. The household is the parent company. The practice is a subsidiary. Every dollar of profit, every decision about reinvestment, every conversation about growth should be evaluated through one primary lens: does this move the household forward?

Household First is not anti-business. It is not about stripping the practice bare or neglecting your team or your patients. It is about making deliberate, intentional decisions that ensure the practice is doing what you built it to do: creating freedom, security, and a life worth living for you and your family.

### *What You Will Find in This Book*

Here is the journey you are about to take:

- Chapter 1 establishes the Household First principle and why most owners are running their finances in the wrong sequence.
- Chapter 2 identifies the nine specific prosperity hurdles that keep smart physical therapists financially frustrated, and why none of them are about intelligence.
- Chapter 3 gives you the economic benchmarks of a healthy physical therapy practice so you know exactly what you are building toward.
- Chapter 4 confronts the most common and costly mistake in practice ownership: treating the household as an afterthought.
- Chapter 5 shows you how to run your household like a business, including the Household CFO role, the account structure, and the financial policies that create order and forward progress.
- Chapter 6 redefines financial planning as something you do, not something you buy, and shows you what a real plan actually looks like.

- Chapter 7 walks through the five timeless lessons of successful investing, including the critical difference between investing and speculating.
- Chapter 8 gives you a step-by-step framework for designing your exit while you still love the practice, including how to calculate your wealth gap and build the right exit team.
- Chapter 9 explains why most financial advisors are not equipped to serve practice owners and what an industry-specific advisor actually looks like.
- Chapter 10 gives you one clear, actionable first step to find out exactly where your household stands today.

### *What This Book Will Do for You*

By the time you finish this book, you will have a complete framework for thinking about the relationship between your practice and your household. You will understand what your numbers need to look like, how to build the systems to get there, and what kind of team you need around you to make it happen.

You will also have something that most practice owners never get: a clear, honest picture of where you actually stand financially, and a concrete path for closing the gap between where you are and where you want to be.

This is not a book about working harder. You are already doing that. This is a book about working with more intention, more structure, and a clearer set of priorities so that the extraordinary effort you pour into your practice starts showing up the way it should: in your household, in your freedom, and in your life.

***The goal is not to build a bigger practice.<br>The goal is to build a better life.***

You have invested everything in building something great. It is time to make sure that investment is working for you.

**Let's get started.**

# Chapter 1

# Household First

You've likely built—or are in the process of building—a great practice. The kind with a full schedule of patients, strong revenue, and a growing team. Yet something doesn't feel right. The train isn't completely on the tracks. Your stress is high, your time feels limited, and your financial situation seems unclear and uncomfortable.

You see the financial reports, and while they say you're doing okay, you realize something:

***Success on paper does NOT equal progress at home.***

You didn't start and build this practice just to "get by." And you certainly didn't build it to feel trapped.

### *The Default Path*

The truth is that most practice owners are following a default path. It's the same path so many of your fellow owners have walked—and it's become as powerful as inertia. It operates in the background like a program running on autopilot: it doesn't inspect or think, it just follows orders.

That "unconscious model" tells you to:

- Grow the practice
- Reinvest everything back into practice
- Max out retirement accounts
- Hope it all works out later

This approach is as clear as mud. There are no defined outcomes. Financial targets are non-existent. It's as if you decided to run your business on purpose—and your household by accident.

### *The Core Problem: The Household Is an Afterthought*

When you run your practice, you apply specific business functions to make sure it operates at its best. You start with an overall business strategy. That strategy guides your actions for growth and expansion. You hold routine meetings with your leadership team to keep everyone aligned. You track metrics for financial solvency, production, quality control, marketing, and more.

In other words, you pay attention to your practice.

Here's the real question: Does your household get that same professional attention?

For most owners, the household gets leftovers. The practice takes priority, and the household finances end up unclear, guesswork-driven, and largely unmanaged. You may have the occasional conversation with your spouse about money, but those conversations are infrequent, unplanned, and rarely productive.

***Your household is the most important entity in your life—yet it has the weakest and most disorganized business system applied to it.***

### *The Household Is the Goal—Not the Practice*

Financial success at the household level is the pinnacle. To understand why, think back to why you started the practice in the first place. Beyond the desire to serve your community, there were personal reasons:

- Freedom from being told what to do
- Control over your time and schedule
- Financial security
- Options and opportunities for your family

It may seem like the practice is the primary asset. But the practice is not the goal. The household is the goal. The household is the primary asset—the practice is a supporting asset. Your practice exists to serve your life, not the other way around.

### *The Cost of Getting It Wrong*

It's easy to spot a practice owner who has this backwards. Generally, you'll see high income alongside a very low net worth. You'll see an owner who takes every dollar of profit and, through either necessity or habit, allows it to be consumed back into the practice. Burnout is common, because the owner never fully recognized the value of what they've built and never had an exit plan. Financial anxiety runs high—fear of not being prepared to retire comfortably—even while income remains strong.

***It is possible to win in your practice and lose in your life at the same time.***

### *What "Household First" Actually Means*

Household First does not mean you neglect your practice. It doesn't mean you don't care about your people, your patients, or your legacy. It certainly doesn't mean stripping every dollar from the practice, neglecting your employees, or hoarding everything for yourself.

Household First means:

- Making decisions with household financial progress as the priority

- Having a systematic method of compensating yourself for every role you play in the practice
- Measuring success not just at the practice level, but at the household level: Debt Free, Invested, Free Time, Set for Life

***Household First is not anti-business.***
***It's pro-purpose.***

***Running Your Household Like a Business***

Your household is a business—and you need to run it like one. We dedicate an entire chapter of this book to this concept. Your household needs a CFO. This is someone who can own that role, track the numbers, and manage the system. What does that role look like? What are the responsibilities? How is it tracked?

But most importantly: if your household were a business, would it be well run? We answer all of those questions in that chapter.

Most practice owners are operators inside their business but completely passive when it comes to their personal finances. If you're still not sure whether this applies to you, consider how comfortably you can answer these three questions:

1. *Do you know exactly how much income, assets, and resources you need to be financially free?*
2. *Do you have a system for moving money from the business to the household that isn't just dictated by your CPA?*

3. *How long would your household economically survive if your practice cash flow suddenly dried up?*

### *What This Book Will Show You*

This book will show you how to turn practice success into personal freedom. You will learn:

- How to build an effective household financial system
- How to extract and allocate your practice income
- How to align your practice with your life goals
- How to design a clear exit

The goal isn't to build a bigger practice. The goal is to build a better life.

### *THE TWO MODELS*

**Old Model**

Practice → Income → Expenses → Leftovers → Hope

**Household First Model**

Household Goals → Income Targets → Practice Strategy → Intentional Allocation

# Chapter 2

# Why Smart Physical Therapists Feel Financially Frustrated

Getting through years of physical therapy school is not for the faint of heart. It takes an immense amount of study, practice, and repetition just to get through the program, and then the real learning curve begins once you're actually in practice. It takes grit, determination, and serious intellectual horsepower to be good at this.

So, if you're financially frustrated, it isn't because you're not smart enough. It also isn't some condition you were born with. There's no such thing as a "bad money gene" or some financial disorder you can use to explain away your situation. You can only blame your parents and upbringing for so long.

To say that things are getting harder financially would be an understatement. For the first time in modern U.S. history, the next generation may actually have it harder than the one before. Assigning blame might make us feel better temporarily, but it won't solve anything. We need to recognize the real financial hurdles in front of us, confront them, and attack them. There's no other way through.

99.9% of your financial condition is the result of things YOU are doing. It's an inside job.

As much as we want to blame external forces like government spending, inflation, a bad economy, taxes, and political parties, the truth is that the vast majority of your financial condition comes down to your own decisions and habits. Let's get clear on the specific hurdles that keep practice owners stuck, so they don't become permanent roadblocks to your financial independence.

***Prosperity Hurdle #1***

**Financial Mismanagement**

Whether deliberate or not, financial mismanagement is defined as the incorrect, inefficient, or careless handling of money, and it leads to a worsening financial condition in both the household and the practice. It is the root cause of insolvency and bankruptcy. Look at any family or company that eventually went under, and somewhere along the way, the money was being mismanaged.

Most owners handle money in the wrong sequence. They wait for money to arrive and then figure out where it should go. Proper financial management works the opposite way: you decide where the money is going before it ever hits your bank account. That single shift creates far better control.

If you have no company reserves, struggle to pay your tax estimates, can't afford necessary equipment or new hires, and barely pay yourself beyond your base salary, you have a financial mismanagement problem. The good news: it is completely fixable. But you have to tackle it immediately. Don't wait. Your number one responsibility is the solvency of your practice and your household.

### *Prosperity Hurdle #2*
### Underestimation

How many times have you started a project thinking you had the right amount of time, money, and resources, only to realize you vastly underestimated the job? It happens constantly. Almost every practice owner underestimates how much income, assets, and resources they actually need to run a profitable practice and still take home enough to secure a comfortable retirement.

Your make-or-break monthly revenue number needs to account for 20% going into profit accounts, all operating expenses, and retirement goals that go far beyond what an online calculator or a cookie-cutter financial advisor will give you.

Starting a job and finishing a job never requires the same number of resources.

### *Prosperity Hurdle #3*
### Lack of Strategy

If you look at the most-searched financial topics online, you'll find that people are obsessed with tactics. They believe they can "hack" their way to financial prosperity. But tactics without a solid strategy will leave you drowning in a tsunami of financial information, most of which doesn't even apply to your situation.

Not having a wealth-building strategy rooted in the proper use of your practice to supercharge your retirement goals is a critical mistake. As Sun Tzu wrote in The Art of War: "Tactics without strategy is the noise before defeat."

### *Prosperity Hurdle #4*
### Debt Obligations

Nothing halts financial progress faster than the weight of debt. While debt certainly has a legitimate role, using destructive debt to buy things now that you're forced to pay for later puts you in invisible chains. Choosing to enrich credit card companies and lending institutions instead of your own household is a serious threat to your long-term financial survival.

Know the difference between constructive debt and destructive debt. Only use debt when it expands your assets and increases your cash flow.

### *Prosperity Hurdle #5*
### Inflation

Most people define inflation as a general rise in prices, but that doesn't explain the "why." Simply put, inflation happens when too much money in circulation chases too few goods and services. Nothing actually improves about the house, the car, or the food item. The price goes up simply because more dollars are competing for the same products.

It may feel like a short-term nuisance, but inflation remains one of the greatest long-term threats to your financial condition. As a practice owner, your number one financial goal should be ensuring your household has more than enough to absorb the effects inflation will have on your wealth over time.

### *Prosperity Hurdle #6*
### Taxes

As government obligations increase, the burden consistently falls on productive citizens to bear the expense. That usually means income taxes that are higher and more demanding over time. Combine that with inflation and you can see clearly who the real enemies of a practice owner's financial growth are.

Most CPAs, while well-versed in the tax code, will default to having you pay the maximum amount of tax just to avoid any risk of an audit. But every dollar you send to the government is one less dollar for your family. You have a duty to legally minimize your tax burden, because you will put that money to far better use.

### *Prosperity Hurdle #7*

### Parasitic People

For a practice and household to function well financially, everyone needs to contribute to the forward momentum of the group. When you allow people to live off the production of others without contributing themselves, solvency problems follow. The negative impact of even one parasitic person in your practice or household cannot be overstated.

It's common to see a practice owner's revenue increase 15–20% once they remove a truly toxic person from the equation. People who are well-intentioned, try hard, and produce value in any form deserve to be protected and supported. Those who deliberately harm the group through malicious inactivity or willful incompetence do not.

### *Prosperity Hurdle #8*

### Investment Mistakes

Nobody plans to lose money when they invest. Yet many owners have felt the sting of putting money into something they didn't fully understand, or weren't entirely sure why they were investing in it to begin with.

Investing is a straightforward concept: you're looking for incremental gains with the priority of getting your principal back. You understand the investment, the value it creates, how it generates profit, and how it fits into your overall strategy. When you put money into something solely hoping the price goes up, that's speculation. Not investing.

Investing isn't about guarantees. It's about knowing what you own and why you own it.

### *Prosperity Hurdle #9*
### An Outdated Financial Team

Your CPA, financial advisor, and bookkeeper work for you. Not the other way around. Yet most practice owners have a financial team whose members never talk to each other. There's no coordination, no shared vision, and no unified strategy.

On top of that, the people who helped you get started may not be the right people to get you to the next level. You need a financial team that understands exactly where you want to go and has the infrastructure, resources, and expertise to take you there.

Everyone needs an upgrade now and then. Your financial team is no exception.

### *Final Thoughts*

Every single hurdle covered in this chapter is something that smart, driven, successful physical therapists deal with every day. The frustration you feel is not a personal failure; it is a predictable outcome of a system nobody taught you. They trained you to be an exceptional clinician. Nobody handed you a roadmap for the financial side of running a practice and building a life at the same time.

Awareness without action is just expensive knowledge. Every day that passes without confronting these hurdles is a day the gap between where you are and where you want to be will get a little wider. Financial frustration does not stay static — unfortunately, it compounds. The good news is that compounding works either way, so once you get moving in the right direction, financial progress is expedited.

Before you move to the next chapter, take ten minutes and do this: go back through the nine hurdles and be completely honest with yourself. Which ones are actively working against you right now? Which ones have you been aware of but quietly tolerating? Write them down. Rank them. Own them. You cannot fix what you refuse to see, but once you see it clearly, you have already taken the hardest step.

You built something real. Now it is time to make sure it is working for you.

# Chapter 3

# The Economics of a Healthy Physical Therapy Practice

One of the most difficult transitions in practice ownership is accepting this truth: your clinical skills will only take you so far. To build and sustain a thriving practice, you need to understand the economics behind it.

Your practice is likely your single largest investment. Like any investment, you want to ensure you're getting a proper return, minimizing risk, and maximizing its value to your household. The top practice owners get this. They understand that business growth depends less on their clinical expertise and more on their leadership, their vision, their ability to manage people effectively, and—most importantly—how responsibly they handle the finances to ensure consistent, abundant profit.

Before we get into the key metrics of a financially healthy practice, let's first look at what a well-run, profitable practice looks like from the inside.

### *What a Well-Run Practice Looks Like*

#### Competent and Well-Trained Personnel

Finding and keeping good staff is one of the biggest ongoing challenges in practice ownership. Constant turnover costs thousands of dollars and puts serious strain on your existing team. While improving your hiring process helps, you often won't know the true fit of a new hire for at least 30 days.

What actually determines whether you keep good people and move the bad ones out quickly is your onboarding process. A strong onboarding system includes clearly defined roles and responsibilities, proper training, mentoring, and enough time for the new hire to genuinely assimilate into your culture.

#### Excellent Patient Care and Outcomes

Outcomes are ultimately what matter most. Did the patient get the result they came in for? While 100% positive outcomes aren't possible in any clinical setting, the ideal practice relentlessly pursues the best care available.

That shows up as:

- High patient acceptance on treatment plans

- Patients following through to treatment completion
- Little to no complaints regarding patient care or follow-up
- Clinicians holding themselves to a consistently high technical standard
- Rave reviews that are actively captured and promoted

### Total Scheduling Control

Disorganized scheduling is one of the most preventable sources of lost revenue. In an era of instant communication and AI-powered tools, there is no excuse for scheduling confusion.

A well-run practice:

- Has team members proactively confirming upcoming appointments and booking the next visit before clients leave
- Maintains a low cancellation rate and has an immediate process for rescheduling missed appointments
- Ensures all providers are running on time
- Uses technology to track the schedule and send clients multiple reminders
- Knows exactly how many available slots exist and works to keep them filled as close to capacity as possible

### Optimum Billing and Collections

A private practice must produce more than the cost to deliver care in order to survive and grow, and that revenue must be collected. Money that should have been invoiced and collected—but wasn't—is the single largest hidden expense in most physical therapy practices. If you deliver a service that produces real outcomes, you deserve to be paid for it.

In the ideal practice, billing and collections means:

- An extremely low accounts receivable balance
- Staff who are confident and courteous when asking for payment
- Clear visibility into exactly how much is invoiced and collected each week
- Accurate, up-to-date financial records that are readily accessible
- Fees and service pricing reviewed regularly to stay profitable given local market conditions

**Strategic and Consistent Marketing**

Regardless of how busy the schedule is today; a well-run practice has a marketing system that consistently brings in new clients while deepening relationships with existing ones. That starts with a clear strategy and a reliable method of communicating your value to the community.

This includes:

- An up-to-date, professional website that accurately represents your practice

- A maintained database of current and prospective clients with regular outbound communication
- Active participation in community activities that raise your visibility and reputation
- A referral system that makes it easy and worthwhile for existing clients to send people your way
- A dedicated marketing resource—internal or external—to plan and execute the strategy

### Real Leadership and Team Management

Most people want to work somewhere they feel genuinely valued and believe their work matters. Good compensation is important, but it is rarely the primary motivator for a committed team member. As the owner, your responsibility is to make sure the vision, purpose, and culture of the practice are clearly understood and embraced by everyone on your staff.

A well-led practice:

- Uses performance metrics as a guide, but ensures every team member understands why their role matters
- Has a clear system for bonusing and recognizing people who perform well
- Addresses or eliminates workplace toxicity immediately
- Documents policies and procedures so expectations are never ambiguous

- Reinvests in the business with purpose and growing profitability

### *The 5 Fundamental Financial Metrics*

Every business has benchmarks that indicate its viability and profitability. Here are the five fundamental metrics every PT practice owner and manager should understand—and actively monitor—to keep the practice on track.

### *Metric #1*

### **70% of New Patients Should Be True New Patients**

New patient acquisition is essential for an economically viable practice. But not all "new" patients are the same. A returning patient coming back for a different condition counts as new in your system—but it is not the same as bringing a genuinely new person through your door for the first time. Both matter, and both should be tracked separately.

Your target ratio is 70% true new patients to 30% returning patients presenting with a new issue. Hitting this ratio is a strong indicator that your marketing strategy is working, your referral network is healthy, your community awareness is growing, and your brand is gaining market share.

Patients returning for a new reason is also a positive sign. It reflects strong clinical outcomes, high patient satisfaction, and a reputation that keeps people coming back. But real patient growth—the kind that fuels future scalability and increases your practice valuation—requires a steady pipeline of genuinely new patients.

***If your new patient ratio is running below 70/30, something is off. Your referral sources may be shrinking, your digital presence may be struggling, or competition in your market may be increasing.***

Maintaining this ratio is a reliable indicator of both your external marketing impact and the quality of the patient experience you are delivering internally..

***Metric #2***

**Keep Lower-Tier Payors Under 10% of Total Reimbursement**

To run a profitable physical therapy practice, your reimbursements must consistently exceed the cost of delivering care. That requires an intimate knowledge of your payor mix.

Most practices categorize their payors by quality. Some use a tiered system: "A-tier" for strong payors, "B-tier" for mediocre ones, and "C-tier" for low-paying contracts. Others simply label them good or bad. The method matters less than the discipline: payors at the bottom of your mix should not represent more than 10% of your total reimbursement.

If you are struggling to keep this metric in range, there are concrete steps you can take:

- Negotiate better contract rates with existing payors
- Cultivate referral sources that send patients with stronger payor coverage
- Align lower-payor patients with more efficient internal scheduling to reduce the cost of serving them
- Drop the contract entirely if it is consistently unprofitable and cannot be improved

Regardless of where your payor mix stands today, there is always something actionable you can do to improve the quality of your contracts and protect your margins.

***Metric #3***

**Aim to Collect 100% of Treatment Reimbursement**

This may seem obvious, but far too many owners become complacent or quietly accepting when it comes to collections. Dealing with insurance reimbursors can feel like a David versus Goliath situation—but that does not mean you are helpless, and it does not mean you should accept less than what you are owed.

You need a bulldog mentality when it comes to your revenue cycle. That requires the right people, the right technology, and the right system working together.

True 100% collections is not realistic, but it is the right target to aim for. Missed patient balances, uncollected co-pays, claim denials, underpayments, authorization errors, and weak follow-up are all symptoms of the same underlying problem: wrong people, wrong system, or wrong technology. If you can close those gaps and consistently collect 95–98% of what is owed, you will sustain profitability and ensure your household continues to make financial progress.

***Leaving money on the table is not a billing problem. It is a systems problem. Fix the system.***

*Metric #4*

**Keep Increasing Your Production Utilization Rate Until You Reach 90–95%**

One of the largest hidden expenses in any physical therapy practice is unused capacity. Every unfilled slot is money that could have been earned but wasn't. You have a finite number of patient slots per week. The goal is to push toward a 90–95% production utilization rate.

If you are under that rate right now, do not treat it as a failure. Treat it as an opportunity. Every percentage point of improvement increases the enterprise value of your practice by putting more productive volume through the same fixed cost base. Track it. Push it. And keep increasing it until you hit the 90–95% sweet spot.

Once you consistently reach that level, it is a reliable signal that the practice is ready to look at expansion—a second location, additional providers, or some form of growth activity.

If you are chronically running below 70–75%, the issue typically comes down to one of three things:

- Your front desk needs better training on scheduling protocols and patient retention
- Your therapists need support managing their caseloads more effectively
- Your referral engine needs work—consistent outreach to past patients and referral sources is not optional at this stage

Many owners hesitate to raise production expectations out of fear their associates will start looking elsewhere. The reality is that most associates want to be challenged. As long as the push feels genuine and is connected to them becoming better clinicians who help more patients, they will rise to meet it.

### *Metric #5*
### 5–10% of Collections Should Be Non-Insurance Revenue

Going fully cash-pay is a dream for many practice owners, but it is not a realistic model for most. That does not mean none of your revenue should be cash-based.

Targeting 5–10% of total collections from non-insurance sources is a reasonable and achievable goal for most practices. While it may seem like a small slice, the benefits reach further than the percentage suggests.

A consistent source of cash revenue helps offset the drag from lower-paying insurance contracts, improves cash flow during months when collections are running slow, increases your revenue per patient, and improves patient retention.

Non-insurance revenue can also make better use of existing space and staff capacity, turning underutilized hours into additional income without significant overhead.

Whatever services you choose to offer—wellness programs, performance training, specialized assessment packages, or retail products—building a modest cash-based revenue stream adds real value to your practice and reduces some of the stress that comes with depending entirely on insurance reimbursors.

***A 5–10% cash revenue base is not a side project. It is a buffer, a growth lever, and a sign of a more resilient practice.***

### *Final Thoughts*

You now have a clear picture of what a financially healthy physical therapy practice looks like from the inside out. The six operational pillars, the five key metrics, the specific targets and ranges. This is not theory. These are the benchmarks that separate practices that quietly struggle from practices that grow with purpose and generate real wealth for their owners.

Now it is time to use them.

Before you move to the next chapter, do this: pull your actual numbers and run them against every metric in this chapter. New patient ratio. Payor mix. Collections rate. Utilization. Non-insurance revenue. Write down where you land on each one. Most owners who go through this exercise for the first time are surprised—sometimes pleasantly, more often not. Either way, knowing is always better than guessing.

If your numbers are close to these benchmarks, that is something to be proud of and build on. If they are not, you now have something more valuable than frustration. You have a specific, measurable starting point. You know exactly where the gaps are, and that clarity is the foundation of every improvement that follows.

**A private practice that hits these targets consistently does not just run better. It funds a better life. Read on.**

# Chapter 4

# Stop Treating Your Household as an Afterthought

Once upon a time, there was a physical therapist who had owned their practice for a number of years. They knew from a young age that this was what they wanted to do with their life. They went to school, got good grades, worked their craft, and eventually became an owner. The practice grew and became a true staple of the community.

By every outward measure, this owner had made it. A thriving practice, millions in revenue, a state-of-the-art facility, and glowing reviews. The "Instagram Practice." But something was missing.

One day, someone said to them: "My goodness, you must have zero financial stress. Your debt must be gone, retirement has to be secured, and you probably know exactly what you'll walk away with when you exit."

The owner looked at them, and with complete honesty said: "There are days when I wonder if I'm making any personal financial progress at all. I only take home what's left over."

Unfortunately, for far too many in this profession, that is not a rare story. It is the norm. Everyone gets paid first. Everyone is prioritized over the household. The financial well-being of the owner's own family is, simply put, an afterthought.

**STOP.**

Creating a household that can function economically free from sole reliance on the practice is every owner's dream. To get there, something fundamental has to shift: the way you view the relationship between your practice and your household.

### *Treat Your Household Like a Business*

A business exists to provide goods or services in exchange for the revenue it needs to survive. Your practice does this every day, and it must operate at a profit to continue and expand.

Your household should be viewed as a different kind of business. Think about it: your household has goals and a purpose. It has income and expenses, assets and debts, just like a business. Every investment and asset you own is ultimately designed to benefit the household. All profit produced by those investments flows through to you on a single tax ID number: your Social Security number. Even the U.S. government treats your household as a business entity.

### *Your Household Is the Parent Company*

In the corporate world, there is a concept called the "parent company." This is a company that owns or controls other companies and investments, known as subsidiaries. The parent company directs and manages those subsidiaries and is typically compensated through management fees or profit-sharing arrangements.

Some well-known examples:

- Alphabet is the parent company of Google
- Meta is the parent company of Facebook, Instagram, and WhatsApp
- Berkshire Hathaway is the parent company of Geico, Dairy Queen, and Duracell

Your household is a parent company. It owns your practice, your real estate, your investment and retirement accounts, your bank accounts, and any other valuable property you hold. All of these should eventually produce some form of economic benefit that flows back to the household.

***Your practice exists to serve the household. Not the other way around.***

### *Prioritize Practice Profits to the Household*

Most owners do not have a systematic approach to taking practice profits. They hope there will be enough left at the end of the month or quarter and rarely see the full benefit of the profits their practice reports. The reason is straightforward: a business will naturally try to spend everything it makes, which leaves very little left over.

**The practice exists to serve the needs of the household.**

That means it should be producing enough income to satisfy three core requirements:

- Your current lifestyle costs
- Extra discretionary spending
- Building additional retirement assets

Most owners only take enough from the practice to cover their current lifestyle. The other two get ignored. That is shortsighted, and over time it leads to burnout, frustration, and a retirement that keeps getting pushed further out.

The fix is to treat your profit distribution like an expense. Going back to the parent company model: most parent companies charge a management fee of roughly 10% of gross revenue, taken from the subsidiary every month. You should do the same.

Set up an automatic, systematic transfer of a percentage of your practice revenue every week. For example, if you bring in $25,000 in gross revenue in a given week, $2,500 moves from the business checking account to a personal account. This can be done electronically and is straightforward to set up. From an accounting standpoint, it is treated as a profit distribution.

### *Setting Up Your Wealth Storage Account*

Every owner should establish a personal Wealth Storage Account designed to capture 10% of weekly practice revenue. The money accumulating in this account is not for consumption. It is for investments outside of the practice that can generate retirement cash flow and allow your household to operate independently from the practice over time.

A few important notes on this:

- **Start where you can.** You will likely feel nervous about this at first. That is completely normal. Many owners should not attempt to pull the full 10% right away. Start with an amount that feels manageable, then set it to increase automatically every four weeks. This gradually pressures the practice to grow revenue and stay disciplined about spending.

- **Keep it separate.** Do not hold the Wealth Storage Account under the business name. The most effective approach is to keep it fully separated from the business. Owners who follow this consistently are the ones who accumulate hundreds of thousands of dollars for their households over time.
- **You have earned this.** Some owners wrestle with the idea of taking money from the practice this way. Most physical therapists did not get into this profession to enrich themselves. But far too many overlook the very real risks of business ownership. You are personally liable for what goes wrong: upset clients, regulatory issues, debt obligations. You deserve to be compensated for the risk and leadership you provide every single day.

### *Final Thoughts*

There are several practical ways to begin running your household with the same discipline you apply to your practice:

- Establish a family mission statement
- Assign one person to serve as the Household Chief Financial Officer

- Review family financial statements on a regular schedule
- Establish household financial policies that govern how money is handled
- Set celebration targets for when financial milestones are reached
- Build a coordinated financial team that is aligned with your household goals

Your household is a priority, not an afterthought. It is time to treat its financial condition with the same professionalism, intention, and care that you bring to your practice and your craft every single day.

This is what Household First looks like in practice. Now let's learn how to run your household like a business.

# Chapter 5

# How to Run Your Household Like a Business

Running your household like a business may seem like a foreign concept. But it can be summed up in two words you already know: Home Economics. Not the kind you might have taken in school, which focused on cooking and interior design. The word "economics" is derived from the Greek term *Oikonomikos*, which means "skilled in household management."

Household management is not just about food preparation. At its core, it describes the skills required to effectively run a home or estate, managing all of its resources and finances to create an abundance of time, money, and meaningful experiences. In other words: how well do you handle and grow your wealth to create a thriving household?

If you own a practice, you already know how to do this. You track revenue, manage expenses, hold team meetings, and make strategic decisions every week. There is just a gap between running your business with systems and applying those same systems at home.

For most owners, the household has:

- No system
- No structure
- Limited accountability

It is time to apply the same principles to your household that you apply to your business.

### *No Rules, No Order*

Most households in America run on old habits, emotion, and convenience. The kids have demands that need to be met. Spouses rarely discuss finances unless something goes wrong. Money comes in, money goes out, and there is rarely much left over.

Think back to the early days of your practice, before you had real systems in place. Everyone was doing their own thing. It led to an overworked owner, confusion, and constant friction.

Three things save any organization from that kind of chaos, including a household:

- Policy
- Process
- Discipline

A policy is a rule, a standard, or a decision made in advance. Without policy, you cannot have control. Most households have no financial policies at all, which is why so many struggle with debt, inadequate savings, underfunded retirement accounts, and recurring arguments about money. Most financial mistakes happen in the moment, driven by emotion. The best way to handle money matters is to decide them in advance.

That does not mean creating a restrictive rulebook that drains the joy out of family life. You do not need dozens of policies. You just need enough to keep the household moving forward. When someone violates a policy, there should be accountability. The specifics of how that works in your household are up to you. The point is that simple, clearly communicated financial policies protect the household and make forward progress possible.

Here are five examples of household financial policies to get you started:

***Example:*** Miller Household Financial Policies

**Purpose:** To ensure we have a household that rewards merit, can function and expand, and where everyone understands the role they play in keeping our family able to love, grow, and help other people.

**Policy #1:** ***We will spend less than we earn.*** While the rest of society believes they can have everything now, we will ensure our household stays solvent by not spending more than we bring in. If we want to spend more, we focus on becoming more productive and valuable.

**Policy #2:** ***We do not rely on consumer debt.*** While some debt can be constructive when it expands assets and income, consumer debt destroys our ability to grow by committing our future income to things we could not afford today.

**Policy #3:** ***We direct 10 to 30% of our income toward savings and investments.*** We understand that our ability to work will diminish over time and we cannot rely on a single income stream forever.

**Policy #4:** ***We plan for irregular and unexpected expenses.*** Life is unpredictable. We will always have money set aside to handle surprises so we can respond with calm rather than panic.

**Policy #5:** ***We define spending approval thresholds.*** Large purchases require both parents to be involved in the decision-making process.

These are examples. Build your own. Just remember this: policies remove emotion from financial decisions, and emotion is where most financial mistakes are made.

### *The Household Chief Financial Officer (HCFO)*

As much as people want to believe in the value of group decision-making, years of observation have led to one clear conclusion when it comes to financial matters:

***Financial decision-making is not a group activity. It is a one-person job.***

Look at how group financial decision-making plays out on a national scale. Congress makes spending decisions on behalf of citizens, and the result is over $37 trillion in debt and growing. Any group left unchecked will try to spend everything it has and then some. You have likely seen this in your own practice.

There are always demands placed on your revenue. It takes one focused, accountable person to keep the practice solvent, maintain reserves, and prevent overspending. Your household needs that same kind of leadership. The HCFO is not simply the person who pays the bills.

The HCFO has financial oversight, makes key financial decisions, and drives system execution. This is not about one person controlling another. It is about accountability. The household still sets financial goals together. The HCFO is the person responsible for making sure those goals get accomplished.

You may have heard the term fiduciary. In simple terms, a fiduciary is someone with a legal and ethical responsibility to prudently manage the assets of another person. They have a duty of care and a duty of loyalty. That is exactly what the HCFO role is. They act in the best interest of the household, protect its investments, and ensure it always has enough income to operate.

### *HCFO Responsibilities*

The HCFO role carries a set of clear, ongoing responsibilities:

- Ensuring the household is solvent, meaning income consistently exceeds expenses
- Eliminating consumer debt on a defined schedule
- Increasing overall net worth over time
- Managing taxes properly and on time
- Driving savings and investment systematically
- Coordinating regular financial meetings
- Working with your financial advisor to execute the household financial plan
- Preparing for emergencies before they happen

Someone needs to own this role. If no one owns it, it does not get done.

### *Building the Financial Infrastructure*

Part of the HCFO's job is building a clear structure for where money goes. Remember: you should know where 99% of every dollar is headed before it arrives. The only way to accomplish that is through a system of dedicated accounts.

Keep it simple, but make sure separate accounts exist for the following:

- **Household Operating Account:** All W-2 salary and a portion of owner draws should automatically flow directly into this account. All regular household bills are paid from here: mortgage, food, utilities, and so on. If you have the discipline, run most of these expenses through a rewards credit card and pay the balance in full each month.
- **Reserve Account:** The household should maintain 6 to 12 months of cash, money market funds, or preferably short-term treasuries. This is your buffer for emergencies and unplanned expenses.
- **Wealth Storage Account:** This is where 10% of weekly practice revenue is deposited. Its purpose is to accumulate capital for household investments outside the practice. As the balance grows, it is deployed according to a wealth-building strategy developed with your financial advisors.
- **Tax Account:** This can be held in either the business or personal name. Because practice profits create a household tax liability, a dedicated account ensures you always have enough set aside for quarterly estimated taxes.

Whatever names you give these accounts, build the system. A good system will outperform willpower every single time.

### *Meetings and Metrics*

Meetings should be regular, practical, and tailored to who is in the room. Here is a simple framework:

**Spousal Meetings: Monthly**

- Current cash positions
- Upcoming expenses
- Income updates
- Progress toward short and long-term financial goals
- Any decisions that need to be made

**CPA Meetings: Quarterly**

- Business profit and expense projections
- Tax liability projections
- Tax minimization strategies

**Financial Advisor Meetings: Monthly (if they have direct experience with healthcare practice owners)**

- Business financial statements and production targets
- Household income and retirement targets
- Household debt targets
- Household financial plan implementation
- Major financial decisions

It may seem like a lot of meetings. But what gets scheduled gets managed.

In addition to meetings, your household should track a set of financial KPIs on a regular basis:

- **Net Worth-** Measures total assets minus total liabilities.

- **Effective Tax Rate-** The actual percentage of total income paid to income taxes.
- **Asset Protection Ratio-** Measures how much asset risk exposure to lawsuits
- **Household Debt-to-Assets Ratio-** Measures the amount of total debt vs total assets.
- **Household Liquidity Ratio-** Measures how much in liquid reserves a household maintains.
- **Household Investment Risk Index-** Shows the overall level of investment risk a household holds in all its assets.
- **Practice Valuation-** Overall market value of the practice.
- **Savings and Investment Ratio-** Percentage of income going to savings and investments.
- **Percentage of Estate Plan Completed and Up to Date-** Measures how much of the basic estate plan and its documents are current and up to date.

If any of these KPIs are unclear or you are unsure how to track them, visit www.econologicsfinancialadvisors.com for guidance.

***The Code of the Household Chief Financial Officer***

You are going to face challenges in this role. You will get push back. There will be moments where you question whether you are doing the right thing. That is completely normal for anyone trying to bring real order and intention to their financial life.

When that happens, come back to this. Talk it through with someone you trust. Take a walk. Pause and breathe. You are not alone.

Here are 10 of the 21 points of the Code of the HCFO. The full list is available in our Roadmap.

1. **I will not cause financial problems.** I will solve them.
2. **I will manage the household finances** with common sense and prudence.
3. **I will continually push** for all family members to be productive and competent.
4. **I promise to keep the household solvent** at all times.
5. **I will not procrastinate** and will take action when I am certain it will benefit the financial well-being of the household.
6. **I promise to direct** a substantial portion of annual household income into investments that create cash flow.
7. **I will maintain** the creditworthiness of the household at an excellent level.
8. **I will keep** all financial commitments as promised.
9. **I will only invest** in things I understand, have researched thoroughly, and that align with my values and long-term financial goals.
10. **I will celebrate our financial successes** and above all, will be charitable to those I can truly help.

### *Final Thoughts*

Everything in this chapter comes down to one shift in identity. You are not just a physical therapist, a practice owner, or a provider. You are the financial leader of your household. That role has a name now. It has responsibilities, a code of conduct, and a system behind it. The only question is whether you are going to step into it with the same seriousness you bring to everything else you do.

Most practice owners read something like this and think, "That makes sense. I should do that." And then life gets busy, the practice demands their attention, and the household stays exactly where it was. Do not let that happen here. The cost of waiting is real, even if it is invisible in the short term.

The first and most important step is to formally claim the HCFO role. Decide who holds it, make it official in your household, and begin operating accordingly. Set up the account structure if it is not already in place. Put the first spousal financial meeting on the calendar. These are not complicated steps. They are just steps that require someone to take them.

If you are ready to take this seriously but are not sure exactly where to start or how to apply these principles to your specific situation, that is exactly what the team at Econologics Financial Advisors is here for. Scan the QR code below to schedule a complimentary introductory discovery call with one of our advisors. They specialize in working with physical therapy practice owners and will help you assess where your household stands today and what steps make the most sense for where you want to go.

Your household is a business. It is time to run it like one.

Schedule Your Discovery Call with Econologics Financial Advisors

# Chapter 6

# Financial Planning Is Something You Do, Not Something You Buy

The best way to describe what financial planning is starts with defining what the ideal outcome should look like.

The optimum financial condition for almost any household would include all of the following results:

- An abundance of income coming in from multiple sources
- Freedom from all destructive debt
- A business that is profitable, sustainable, and transferable
- Assets that are protected from taxes, inflation, and lawsuits

- Time and freedom for household members to pursue the life they want to live.

This is the household in its most economically healthy form. It is not defined purely by net worth. It is an outcome built on structure, discipline, and behavior that produces stability, control, and real freedom of choice.

When you get clear on what your optimum condition looks like, you can honestly evaluate where you stand today and identify exactly what needs to change. The only way to move from your current condition to your ideal one is to have a blueprint that bridges the gap between the two.

That is where a financial plan comes in.

A financial plan is a roadmap for getting from where you are to where you want to be. It should include clearly defined financial goals, key metrics, the core areas that need to be addressed, specific action steps, and someone accountable to help you implement it. Financial planning is a process, a discipline, and a behavioral system that allows you to methodically close the gap between your current reality and your ideal financial life.

**99% of practice owners think they have a financial plan. The evidence says otherwise.**

***The Illusion of Being Planned***

The financial industry has put far too much emphasis on selling financial products and far too little on building actual structure. As a result, most practice owners have been led to believe they are more prepared than they are.

Here is what we commonly hear:

- "I have a financial guy I meet with once or twice a year."
- "I have a retirement account, so I have a plan."
- "I have insurance, so I am protected."

The truth is that most owners do have:

- Assets
- Investments
- Insurance policies
- A financial professional

What they do not have is a strategy. It is not uncommon to meet an owner who has 12 accounts, 3 insurance policies, and no clear idea why they own any of it or what the end goal is supposed to be.

You can sense when something is missing because you are the one being forced to figure it all out yourself. Consider this: if you were tasked with building a state-of-the-art physical therapy facility, would you design it yourself from scratch? Or would you hire an architect who has done it before and knows exactly what they are doing? The answer is obvious. Financial planning is no different.

Tactics are what most people end up doing when they purchase financial products. They buy investments, insurance policies, tax structures, and whatever other tools seem relevant. That is not a plan.

Strategy is something different entirely. Strategy means setting clear objectives, establishing financial priorities, building cash flow, managing risk, and defining timelines and targets. Tactics without strategy is just noise.

### *The Architecture of Financial Planning*

A real financial plan is built on six components:

1. **A Financial Architect**

   You need a qualified financial advisor who can help you create, maintain, and monitor your financial progress. That person should:

   - Be a Registered Investment Advisor with a clean record
   - Have deep, hands-on knowledge of the business side of your specific industry
   - Be able to provide case studies showing how they have helped other owners achieve financial success
   - Understand exit planning
   - Use household financial metrics to measure progress over time

2. **Vision Design**

   This is where you define what you are working toward:

- Clearly defined financial objectives
- Income targets
- Business targets
- Retirement targets
- Legacy planning

3. **Financial Management Design**

This addresses how money moves through both the practice and the household:

- Where it comes from
- Where it is going
- How it is stored
- How it is invested

4. **Risk Management Design**

This covers every area that could create financial losses for the household:

- Personal risk
- Practice risk
- Market risk
- Legal risk
- Inflation risk

5. **Tax Management Design**

This ensures the household is always optimizing its tax position:

- Filing on time and in full compliance

  - Quarterly estimates paid
  - Legal tax avoidance strategies
  - Proactive tax planning year-round

6. **Control Systems**

   This ensures the owner has complete visibility and oversight over their entire financial life:

  - Regular reporting
  - Monthly financial reviews
  - Measurable benchmarks
  - Clear accountability
  - Automation wherever possible

Real financial planning is not a static document you file away and forget. It is a regular cadence of meetings with your financial advisor that keeps you focused, accountable, and consistently implementing the strategies that move your household forward.

***The Cost of Not Planning***

Life has a way of punishing inaction. There is no such thing as staying the same financially. You are either moving forward or sliding backward. Not planning for your future is itself a choice, and it carries real consequences:

- Burnout
- Permanent dependency on practice income
- Forced exits on someone else's timeline

- Delayed freedom
- An underfunded retirement
- Ongoing decision fatigue

***Financial planning is not something you buy. It is something you build, practice, execute, and live.***

### *Final Thoughts*

Most practice owners have spent years accumulating financial products without ever building a financial plan. They have accounts, policies, and advisors, but no strategy connecting any of it. If that describes your situation, the good news is that you now know exactly what has been missing and what needs to change.

Stop buying. Start building.

The six components covered in this chapter are not a checklist you hand off to someone else. They are the foundation of a financial life that actually works in your favor. And the single most important step you can take right now is finding a financial advisor who genuinely understands the world you operate in. Not a generalist. Not someone who treats your practice like any other small business. Someone who has worked with physical therapy practice owners specifically and knows how to align your practice economics with your household goals.

Before you move to the next chapter, do two things. First, go back through the six architecture components and honestly assess what you have in place and what you do not. That gap analysis will tell you more about your real financial condition than most owners ever take the time to find out. Second, if you do not already have the right advisor in your corner, do not wait.

The team at Econologics Financial Advisors works exclusively with healthcare practice owners and is built to help you design a real plan, not sell you products. Scan the QR code below to schedule a complimentary discovery call and find out exactly where you stand.

In Chapter 7, we take a close look at investment strategy and walk through the core principles that will help you build enough wealth to never worry about running out of money.

Schedule Your Discovery Call with
Econologics Financial Advisors

# Chapter 7

# The 5 Timeless Lessons of Successful Investing

Financial success comes down to three core skills: knowing how to acquire money, how to control money, and how to invest money.

We tend to overcomplicate investing. We look at the likes of Warren Buffett or the giants of Wall Street and assume we could never match their intellect or training on the subject. However, that is not what smart investing requires.

You do not need to be a hedge fund manager to be a savvy investor. What you need is the ability to see through the noise of bad information that floods this subject every day. Everyone has an opinion on where you should put your money. Most of that advice comes from people with a vested financial interest in your decision and no real accountability for the outcome.

### *Investment Myths*

Before we get into the core lessons, let us clear up some popular investment myths. Remember: every myth contains a grain of truth. There are no absolute rules when it comes to investing, no one holds the holy grail, and blanket generalizations are usually a warning sign.

#### *Myth #1*

#### Higher Returns Always Mean Better Investing

**Reality:** Most people are so fixated on returns that they completely ignore the risk required to achieve them, the tax inefficiency involved, and the illiquidity of the investment.

Most high returns come down to good timing. Even gamblers get lucky.

#### *Myth #2*

#### The Stock Market Is the Only Way to Build Real Wealth

**Reality:** There is nothing wrong with investing intelligently in public securities. But the truth is that the majority of your wealth will be determined by how well you run your practice, how disciplined you are in saving and investing, how effectively you use leverage to acquire real estate, and how much you keep through smart tax planning.

*Myth #3*

**All Insurance Products Are Bad Investments**

**Reality:** Most insurance-based strategies, when structured properly, are excellent risk management, tax planning, and liquidity tools. They are not growth vehicles, and they were never meant to be. The problem is not the product itself. It is the misuse of the product through improper design and application.

*Myth #4*

**Diversification Means Owning More Funds**

**Reality:** We regularly see clients with 12 different funds that all own essentially the same underlying investments. Most people have no idea how much overlap exists in their portfolio. Owning more is not the same as being diversified.

*Myth #5*

**I Need to Build Multiple Income Streams Right Now to Be Financially Free**

**Reality:** The ultimate goal is to have five or six income sources flowing to the household. But the sequence matters enormously. Your first responsibility is to get one income stream running like the Mississippi River. That stream is your practice. Once the practice is truly viable, you take a portion of that income and begin building other streams. Trying to build everything at once before the foundation is solid is one of the most common and costly mistakes practice owners make.

Just because you hear something from an investment guru does not mean it applies to your situation. Inspect the advice, stay anchored to your financial goals, and keep trusted people around you to help make sound decisions.

***What Is an Investment? Really.***

Before we get into the five lessons, it is worth making sure we are working from the same definitions. It is hard to learn something well without a clear understanding of what it really is.

According to Benjamin Graham and David L. Dodd in their book "Security Analysis", an investment operation is defined as "one which, upon thorough analysis, prioritizes safety of principal and an adequate return."

Read that carefully. It does not say 12%, 15%, or 35% annual return. It says adequate, meaning enough to protect your purchasing power. And it emphasizes the safety of your principal above all else, meaning getting your money back.

Now contrast that with speculation: Speculation is an activity where the objective is high returns based on price movements and market sentiment, with little to no concern for the underlying value of what is being purchased.

The most dangerous place you can be financially is when you are speculating while believing you are investing. If you bought a stock only hoping the price would go up, with no understanding of the company behind it, you were speculating.

There is nothing inherently wrong with speculation, as long as you understand the difference, approach it correctly, and only put in an amount you can genuinely afford to lose.

> **The Wrong Way to Speculate:**
> You see Bitcoin up 150% and hear people making millions. Every indication says it will keep going. You pull $50,000 from your business checking account and buy in.
>
> **The Right Way to Speculate:**
> You spend months reading about cryptocurrency and Bitcoin specifically. You read the Bitcoin White Paper. You study the underlying value proposition. You analyze whether the current price reflects real demand or market mania. You review your existing portfolio and determine how much exposure to this type of volatile asset makes sense. You decide to dollar-cost average, buying a set amount each month.

You have a responsibility to your family, your practice, and yourself to invest prudently. You work too hard to claim ignorance or hand full responsibility to someone else. That does not mean you need to manage your own asset allocation, execute trades, or handle rebalancing. Working with a qualified advisor is not just acceptable, it is smart. But that advisor needs to look beyond your retirement accounts. Your investment strategy must be inclusive of all household assets: your practice, real estate, bank accounts, and everything else. An advisor who understands how your practice is valued, what its profit margins should look like, and how it contributes to your household is not optional. It is essential.

***You need to know WHAT you own and WHY you own it.***

***Lesson #1***

**Having an Investment Policy Is More Important Than Short-Term Performance**

Think back to the early days of your practice before you had any real policies in place. Remember the chaos, the reactive decision-making, the fires you were constantly putting out. Now think about how much that costs you, financially speaking.

The same dynamic plays out with personal investing. Most people who lose money or consistently underperform do so for one primary reason: they never created an investment policy to govern how they allocate the profits they take home.

A Household Investment Policy is a document that outlines the rules for how your household invests. It includes:

- The short and long-term goals the investments are designed to serve
- The level of risk the household is willing to assume
- An accountability team that includes advisors, money managers, and household members
- The types of investments the household will and will not participate in
- The overall allocation of assets across categories
- A structured framework for making investment decisions

This policy acts as a circuit breaker. It keeps household members from acting impulsively, panic-selling when markets drop, or handing money to unvetted investment schemes with a high probability of loss.

In short, a Household Investment Policy Statement defines the purpose of the investment, how much risk you want to take, how the money will be managed, and what you plan to do when things go sideways.

***Calm decisions are the foundation of successful investing.***

***Lesson #2***

**The Value of Any Investment Is a Function of the Price You Paid for It**

To understand this lesson, you need to clearly distinguish between two terms: price and value.

Price is what you pay. It is driven by market sentiment, investor emotion, available liquidity, and supply and demand.

Value is what you get.

Consider two investors buying the same rental property:

- Investor A pays $500,000 and collects $30,000 per year in rent. Return on investment: 6%.
- Investor B pays $400,000 for the same property, collects the same $30,000 per year in rent. Return on investment: 7.5%.

The asset is identical. But the investment provides significantly more value to Investor B simply because they paid a better price.

It is entirely possible to buy the best company in the world and get very little value from it because you overpaid. When you pay too much, you leave yourself no margin of safety. The company must perform flawlessly for years just for you to break even.

None of us can predict exactly how any investment will perform. But the price you pay is one of the few things you can truly control. Be mindful of it.

***Lesson #3***

**Buying Something Only for Its Return Is Like Getting Married Only for the Looks**

We all like to think we are not superficial. But most of us have made the mistake of judging someone by appearance only to be genuinely surprised once we got to know them. The same bias shows up in how people choose investments.

Judging an investment purely on its return is one of the leading causes of investor underperformance. Study after study shows how poorly individual investors perform relative to the major market indices. When you evaluate something based only on what it has returned, you set yourself up for disappointment. Strong recent returns are almost always driven by temporary demand or investor euphoria, neither of which lasts. And by the time most people enter the investment, the best of the return has already been captured by someone else.

Instead, look for:

- Important companies with a meaningful role in their industry
- Profitable companies with strong and consistent earnings
- Companies with little to no debt
- Companies that pay and grow dividends
- All-of-the-above purchased at a reasonable or discounted price

This approach does not just improve your odds of investment success. It gives you a genuine understanding of what you own and why you own it. That depth of understanding is what keeps you steady when markets get turbulent.

### *Lesson #4*

### The Greatest Investment Successes Are Built on Concentration

Most practice owners have been trained to believe in diversification as the first rule of investing. Spread it around. Do not put all your eggs in one basket. Minimize risk by owning everything.

That is not how significant wealth is built. Most of the names on the Forbes billionaire list are not there because they had perfectly diversified portfolios. They got there by concentrating their effort and capital into one area and executing at a high level.

As a practice owner, your largest concentration of wealth is almost certainly your practice. If you are treating it as the investment asset it is, the value of your practice likely represents more than 50% of your household net worth. If you also own the real estate where the practice operates, that concentration could be 60 to 70% of your total net worth. That is not a problem. That is an advantage.

Concentration gives you control. How well you manage, grow, and eventually exit your practice will have a greater impact on your retirement than almost any other financial decision you make. The proceeds from a well-timed practice sale can provide an enormous retirement buffer that reduces stress and preserves freedom.

The smartest practice owners also make sure they are pulling a portion of practice revenue along the way to build investment assets outside the practice. A target of 7 to 10% of practice revenue should be directed into an investment strategy, paid to the household as a profit distribution on a weekly basis, and used solely for investment purposes.

Diversification becomes most important after you sell the practice. That is the point when you will want a professional financial advisor or wealth manager to construct a portfolio designed to minimize loss and generate reliable cash flow for the household.

***Diversification matters most after you sell. Until then, concentration is your greatest advantage.***

### *Lesson #5*

### Always Maintain Strategic Liquidity

Healthcare practice owners tend to accumulate wealth in illiquid assets. This typically includes:

- Practice equity
- Medical office real estate
- Other private investments

These assets can grow significantly over time, but they cannot be converted to cash quickly when you need it.

There is a useful way to think about emergencies: they are predictable occurrences that happen at unpredictable times. You do not know when, but you know they are coming.

As a practice owner, you can count on eventually facing:

- A key employee leaving without warning
- A weather event or unexpected closure temporarily shutting down the practice
- Critical equipment breaking down
- A legal action or regulatory matter
- An economic or social event impacting practice revenue

You will also encounter opportunities that require fast capital:

- Discounted real estate
- A chance to acquire another practice
- Buying out a partner's shares

The probability of all of these occurring at some point in your ownership lifetime is high. What you cannot predict is the timing. Both emergencies and opportunities require fast access to capital. Liquidity is what gives you freedom and negotiating power when it counts most.

***Liquidity Framework***

Build your liquidity in three layers:

1. **Personal Reserves:**

   Maintain enough liquidity at the household level to cover 6 to 10 months of living expenses. This is your first line of defense.

2. **Business Reserves:**

   At a minimum, carry two months of business operating reserves. The target should be five to six months.

3. **Credit Lines:**

   Establish open lines of credit while your financial position is strong. This includes a business line of credit, a home equity line of credit, a securities-backed line of credit, or cash value from a life insurance policy. Banks do not lend generously to people in distress. Set these up before you need them.

***Your illiquid assets are there to help you build wealth. Your liquidity is there to protect it.***

### *Final Thoughts*

Investing is not complicated. It has been made to feel that way by an industry that profits from your confusion. The five lessons in this chapter are not advanced strategies reserved for Wall Street professionals. They are timeless principles that any practice owner can apply right now to start making smarter, calmer, and more intentional decisions with their money.

But knowing the principles and then actually living by them are two different things. So, before you move on, take a few minutes and do this honestly.

First, ask yourself: Do you know what you own and why you own it? Not in a general sense. For every account, every policy, every fund, and every investment in your portfolio, can you clearly explain what it is, what role it plays in your overall strategy, and what outcome it is working toward? If the answer is no (for even a handful of items), that is where you should start.

Second, do you have a Household Investment Policy in writing? Not in your head. Written down, agreed upon, and followed consistently. If you do not, you are making investment decisions without guardrails, and that is how good income earners end up with disappointing results.

Work through both of those exercises. Be honest about what you find. If you discover gaps that feel too big to tackle on your own, the team at Econologics Financial Advisors has the tools and resources to help you build a strategy that connects your investments to your practice, your household, and the life you are working toward.

Your money should be working as hard as you do. These five lessons are how you make sure it does.

# Chapter 8

# Designing Your Exit While You Still Love the Practice

Remember when you were young and someone said, "Let's go do something we have never done before!" You were probably excited, nervous, and a little anxious, but completely willing to jump into the adventure. There is nothing wrong with starting something with no idea how it will turn out.

When most physical therapy practice owners decided to open their practice, that is exactly what they did. For many, the decision was driven by a desire to control their own destiny and never work for someone else again. There is a honeymoon phase early on, where the motivation is high and every morning feels like a chance to build something meaningful.

But the novelty does eventually wear off. After enough years of managing staff, handling overhead, fighting regulatory headaches, and carrying the weight of ownership, something shifts. The passion that drove you to build starts to quietly fade. It does not happen overnight. It is a slow accumulation of losses, frustrations, and unmet expectations that chip away at the energy you started with.

You still show up. You still give 100% to your patients. You still pay the bills. But the drive to grow and expand is gone, and you start looking for a way out.

This is why most practices get stuck in neutral. It has very little to do with the economy, the staff, annoying clients, or external circumstances.

***You simply fell out of love with your practice.***

The way to get that feeling back is to change how you relate to the practice.

### *Treat Your Practice as an Investment*

You have probably heard the sayings: "Don't serve the business, make the business serve you" and "Work on the business, not in the business." Both are true. But there is another layer that often gets overlooked: your practice is not just a place you go to help patients and fulfill your purpose. It is also the most powerful wealth-building engine you will ever have access to.

When you decide to treat the practice as an investment, you commit to doing everything possible to maximize its value so that when you eventually transition to the next phase of your life, you can convert that investment into the household security and freedom you have been working toward.

That makes complete sense in theory. The problem is that most practice owners have no real idea what their practice is worth on the open market. Most say the sale proceeds will be a significant part of their retirement plan, yet they have never calculated what they actually need, and they have no clear picture of what role the exit will play in their post-sale financial life.

Even more concerning: most owners have never written an exit plan. Not a rough outline. Nothing. The day-to-day demands of running the practice and managing family responsibilities crowd out the long-term thinking that would make the exit far less stressful and far more profitable.

***No matter where you are on your ownership journey, the time to start planning your exit is today.***

The investment of time you make now will pay off in ways that are difficult to fully appreciate until you are sitting across the table from a buyer. Here are the five steps to designing a smart exit.

### *Step #1*

### Know Your Options

From a macroeconomic standpoint, there has rarely been a better time to own and exit a profitable physical therapy practice. Well-run practices are selling at higher multiples than at almost any point in the last 40 years. As long as demand for physical therapy services remains strong and capital continues to flow into the healthcare space, values are likely to remain favorable.

But options matter. Before reviewing them, there are two foundational questions you need to answer honestly:

- Is the season of practice ownership over for you?
- Are you financially prepared to give up the annual cash flow the practice provides?

If you can answer both with a confident yes, here are your primary exit options:

> **Option #1: Die with Your Boots On:** Not recommended, but more common than it should be. This is typically the path of an owner who struggled to let go and had persistent challenges with delegation and personnel management.
>
> **Option #2: Close the Doors:** Also, not ideal. This usually happens when an owner faces financial difficulties, cannot find qualified associates, or has simply run out of energy for the game.

**Option #3: Gift to Your Children:** Many owners dream of passing the practice to their kids. Fewer than 5% manage to do it successfully. If this is your plan, it requires intentional preparation well in advance.

**Option #4: Sell to a Competitor:** There are likely other providers in your area who would love to acquire what you have built. Be mindful of how you handle professional relationships throughout your career. You may be eliminating a future buyer by burning bridges along the way.

**Option #5: Sell to an Associate or Internal Buyer:** If you invest in your associates, train them well, and give them a vision for their future, you may find your best exit is already inside your building.

**Option #6: Sell to Corporate:** It is the least favorite option for most independent owners, yet it is the most common exit for one reason: corporate buyers tend to pay the most. One important warning: never structure a corporate exit where your retirement depends on the second bite of the apple. It rarely works out the way it is presented.

Regardless of which option fits you best, any serious buyer will pay for the same things: a practice that generates consistent free cash flow, is not dependent on one person, has a strong team, and is free of regulatory issues. Build something profitable, sustainable, transparent, and transferable, and you will never have trouble finding a buyer.

### *Step #2*

### Know Your Numbers

According to CNBC, more than 56% of Americans do not know how much they need to retire comfortably. 51% believe they will outlive their savings. And 35% have done nothing to address it.

Half the country is worried. A third are doing nothing about it. Do not be in either group.

Part of what drew you to practice ownership was the belief that you could achieve more than a standard retirement and do it faster than conventional financial advice would suggest. Here is the math that makes that possible.

### *The Math*

The calculation is straightforward:

> **Determine your Desired Income**
>
> How much monthly income do you need to feel completely satisfied and cover your ideal lifestyle? Be honest and be specific.
>
> Example: **$20,000 per month ($240,000 per year)**
>
> **Calculate your Total Asset Base**

This is the total amount of assets needed to generate your Desired Income. It is not limited to retirement or brokerage accounts. It includes real estate, business interests, and all other income-producing assets. To arrive at this number, multiply your Desired Income by 20.

Example: **$240,000 x 20 = $4,800,000 Total Asset Base needed**

This means you would need $4,800,000 in cash-flow-generating assets at a 5% return to cover your $240,000 annual income need. Note: exclude your primary residence from this calculation, as it does not generate income in most cases.

### *Step #3*

### Close the Wealth Gap

Once you know your Total Asset Base target, the next step is to honestly assess where you stand today. Pull your personal net worth statement. Add up the value of all your assets: practice value, retirement accounts, bank accounts, real estate, and other investments. Subtract the value of your primary home.

**Example:**

| | |
|---|---:|
| Net practice value (after debt and taxes): | $2,000,000 |
| Retirement accounts: | $ 750,000 |
| Real estate: | $ 900,000 |
| **Total Current Assets:** | **$3,650,000** |

*Therefore:*

| | |
|---|---|
| Total Asset Base Needed: | $4,800,000 |
| Current Asset Base: | $3,650,000 |
| **Wealth Gap:** | **$1,150,000** |

The Wealth Gap is the difference between what you need and what you currently have. It tells you exactly what needs to happen before you can exit with confidence.

There are three ways to close it:

1. **Increase your savings from the practice.** If you are only moving $40,000 per year from the practice into household investment accounts, that number needs to increase. Revisit Chapter 4 for a refresher on the mechanics of pulling more profits out of the practice consistently.
2. **Increase the value of the practice.** Because a physical therapy practice is valued on a multiple of its profit, typically 6 to 8 times, every additional dollar of net profit multiplies in value. Add $100,000 in net profit and your practice value potentially increases by $600,000 to $800,000.
3. **Invest prudently.** The biggest financial risk you face is losing money you have already earned. Do not put hard-earned profits at risk by chasing things you do not fully understand. Your practice is already your highest-risk asset.

***Closing your Wealth Gap year by year is the target.***

***Taking action now is what makes an anxiety-free retirement possible.***

*Step #4*

**Build Your Exit Team**

Trying to navigate the exit process alone would be like trying to build the Great Pyramid by yourself. The number of moving parts involved in exit planning is too large for one person to manage.

You need a coordinated team of specialists. Here are the key players:

**Industry-Based Mergers and Acquisitions Broker**

This is the person who helps you cross the finish line. They find buyers, lead negotiations, and execute the best overall deal, not necessarily just the highest price. Industry experience is non-negotiable here.

**Industry-Based CPA**

Your CPA will calculate the tax liability on the sale and ensure your financial statements are clean and credible. They are essential for giving buyers the financial visibility they need and for helping you understand the true after-tax proceeds.

**Business Attorney**

Expensive, yes. Optional, no. A transaction of this size requires a competent attorney to review every legal document before you sign anything.

**Industry-Based Business Consultant**

You are building your practice to fit your ideal exit. A consultant who has been through this process personally, or has guided other owners through it, is an invaluable resource for making sure you are building the right things before you go to market.

**Industry-Based Registered Investment Advisor**

How you handle the sale proceeds is just as important as the sale itself. There is too much money on the line to work with someone who does not have a clear plan for your household cash flow, prudent investment of the proceeds, tax minimization, asset protection, estate planning, and ongoing monitoring of all household investments. You want an advisor who has helped dozens of healthcare practice owners navigate the full exit process from start to finish.

### *Step #5*

### Know How You Will Spend Your Time When the Practice Is Gone

As a practice owner, your mind is running at full speed constantly. You are always thinking, planning, managing problems, and trying to deliver the best possible experience for your patients and team. When you sell and that all stops, the sudden deceleration can be jarring in ways people rarely anticipate.

If you do not have something meaningful to replace the purpose that practice ownership gave you, the void can lead to restlessness, poor habits, and an overall decline in well-being. You earned the leisure. But too much unstructured time without purpose is its own kind of problem.

Before you exit, develop a clear vision of what your life looks like on the other side. Travel, part-time work, mentoring, volunteering, creative pursuits, more time with family. The more concrete that picture is, the smoother the transition will be. You just secured your financial life. Make sure you have a plan to enjoy your retirement.

### *Final Thoughts*

Do not be afraid to negotiate hard on every aspect of the sale. That includes your employment agreement if you stay on after closing, the lease terms on the building (always push for an annual step-up clause and a five-to-ten-year renewal option), and the overall sales price if your revenue numbers continue to grow during the buyer's due diligence phase. Everything is negotiable. Act like it.

Keep the sale confidential until it is the right time to disclose. When word gets out that you are selling for a significant sum, you will quickly discover how many people suddenly have strong opinions about what you should do with the money. Some of them will be very convincing. Be cautious. There is a reason so many athletes and celebrities go broke quickly after a windfall. Do not let that be your story.

One more important reality check: the sale proceeds will almost never generate the same level of annual income that the practice produces while you are actively running it. Before you sign anything, make absolutely sure the sale will provide more than enough to secure your household for life, not just cover it.

***You got this.***

In the next chapter, we take an honest look at why most financial advisors working with healthcare practice owners are simply not providing what you need to win.

# Chapter 9

# Why Your Financial Advisor Sucks

That title might sting a little. Let me explain.

This is not a blanket statement that all financial advisors are bad at their jobs. Most of them are smart, well-intentioned professionals who genuinely want their clients to succeed. The problem is not their intelligence or their character. The problem is that the service model most advisors operate under simply does not match the actual needs of a physical therapy practice owner.

Most of you did everything right when you first hired a financial advisor. You found someone reputable, probably referred by someone you trust or affiliated with a well-known firm like Edward Jones, Ameriprise, Merrill Lynch, or Northwestern Mutual. You started contributing to retirement and brokerage accounts. You have likely been doing this for years.

And yet something still feels off:

- You do not feel fully prepared
- You do not feel in control
- You do not really know your numbers
- Your household still feels disconnected from the growth happening in your practice

You do not have a bad advisor. You have an incomplete one.

***The Standard Advisor Playbook and Why It Falls Short***

Most of your experience with financial advisors has been shaped by what they are trained to do. They set up retirement accounts, IRAs, and 401(k)s. The standard advice is to max them out and you will be fine. They allocate your investments across a portfolio of stocks, bonds, mutual funds, and ETFs. They meet with you once or twice a year, show you performance charts against market benchmarks, and maybe discuss some insurance products along the way.

That is investment management. It is not the same as helping you manage your financial life.

What is missing? Cash flow strategy. Tax planning. Exit planning. A system for handling the income variability that comes with practice ownership. None of those are part of the standard playbook.

There is a practice-to-household disconnect that most financial advisors do not even recognize as a problem. They treat you like a W-2 employee. But the reality of your situation is very different. Why?

- Your practice is your largest asset by a wide margin.
- Your income is irregular, complex, and unstructured, nothing like a salary.
- Your financial risk is highly concentrated in one business.

Your advisor is optimizing the 10% of your wealth that sits in managed accounts while effectively ignoring the other 90%.

***You outgrew them. They just never told you.***

### *What Differentiates an Industry-Specific Advisor*

Not all financial advisors are the same. Here is what separates one built for your world from one who is not.

### *Differentiator #1*

### **They Understand How You Actually Make Money**

An average advisor sees your salary. An industry-specific advisor understands your entire economic picture:

- What your production targets should be and how much needs to be collected to hit them
- The different methods of owner compensation and how to systematically pull profits to the household
- Seasonality patterns in your revenue and what to do to prevent cash flow crunches
- The specific economics of physical therapy practice ownership and what it takes to stay solvent and grow

### *Differentiator #2*

### They Integrate the Practice into the Household Plan

An average advisor focuses on maxing out your retirement contributions. An industry-specific advisor connects the practice and the household into a single, coordinated financial plan.

They show you:

- How much to leave in the practice versus how much to take home at any given time
- When to reinvest back into the practice and when to extract cash for the household
- How practice growth directly impacts your personal financial trajectory

### *Differentiator #3*

### They Understand the Full Lifecycle of a Practice Owner

Most advisors tell you to worry about the exit when

you are ready to retire. An industry-specific advisor starts planning for it long before that.

They look at:

- The growth and scale trajectory of your practice
- What your practice is worth today and what is driving that value
- What needs to happen between now and exit to maximize what you walk away with
- Which exit options are realistic for your situation
- Whether you are financially prepared to leave when you want to

***This is your biggest payday. Do not hope for a good exit. Engineer one.***

*Differentiator #4*

**They Build a Household System, Not Just a Portfolio**

An average advisor manages your retirement investments and tracks your progress toward replacing 70% of your income. An industry-specific advisor builds a full household financial system.

That means:

- Showing you how much you are actually keeping after taxes, expenses, and reinvestment
- Calculating your personal burn rate so you know exactly what your lifestyle costs
- Ensuring you have a sufficient and consistent savings strategy

- Managing multiple investment buckets with different purposes and timelines
- Building a tax-aware distribution plan, not just an accumulation strategy
- Designing a retirement plan built around income and cash flow, not just a net worth number

***You do not live on your net worth.***
***You live on cash flow.***

***Differentiator #5***

**They Are Proactive, Not Calendar-Driven**

An average advisor schedules two meetings a year, reviews market performance, adjusts your allocation, and sends you a quarterly statement. An industry-specific advisor operates on a meeting cadence built around what you actually need.

At a minimum, that means monthly engagement covering both business and personal finances, including:

- Profit analysis
- Income projections
- Expansion planning
- Personal financial KPI reviews

More importantly, they are available to help you answer the questions that actually keep you up at night:

- Can I afford to make this decision right now?
- Should I be pulling more out of the business or leaving it in?

- Am I on track to step away when I want to?

### *The Bottom Line*

Your current advisor probably means well. They are likely smart and genuinely want you to do well. The gap between what you have and what you need is not about intelligence or effort on either side.

***The difference is that one advisor is built for your world. And the other one is not.***

### *Final Thoughts*

Your current advisor probably means well. They are likely smart and genuinely want you to succeed. But good intentions and the right service model are two different things. The gap between what you have and what you need is not a reflection of their character. It is a reflection of whether they were built for y our world.

Use the five differentiators in this chapter as a measuring stick. Go through them one by one and honestly assess where your current advisor stands.

Ask yourself these questions:

- Do they understand how a physical therapy practice generates money and how to structure that income to you as the owner?
- Do they integrate the practice into your household plan?

- Do they have a clear exit strategy mapped out for you, or is that a conversation that never comes up?
- Are they proactively engaged in your financial life, or do you mostly hear from them twice a year around tax season?

If you find yourself answering no to most of those questions, that is not a personal failure on anyone's part. It is useful information. And it tells you exactly what kind of advisor you need to be looking for.

The team at Econologics Financial Advisors was built specifically for practice owners like you. They understand the full picture: the practice, the household, the exit, and everything in between. If you want to find out what a truly industry-specific financial plan looks like for your situation, scan the QR code below to schedule a complimentary discovery call. No pressure. Just clarity.

***One advisor is built for your world.***
***Make sure yours is that one.***

Schedule Your Discovery Call with Econologics Financial Advisors

# Chapter 10

# Make a Power Move

***Financial success is virtuous, ethical, and righteous.***

Congratulations. You have made it through what may be the first book you have ever read that shows you how to put your household first and build your practice to serve your life. That is not a small thing. You have confronted some hard truths about how you have been handling your personal finances, and you now have a better framework to operate from.

But here is where most people stop. They feel motivated, close the book, and do nothing. Life gets busy, the practice demands their attention, and two months later nothing has changed.

***If nothing changes after reading this book, then this book did not help you.***

Healthcare practice owners have never had more opportunities available to them. But those opportunities will only be captured by the ones who stop delaying. The easiest path is to keep telling yourself you are too busy or not ready to make the commitment. There is a graveyard full of practice owners who repeated those thoughts, stayed stuck in the mud, and watched years pass with no real financial progress. Do not be in that group.

We are not asking you to fully commit to a philosophy or system just yet. We are asking you to take one first step: find out where you stand.

### *You Measure Everything at Work. What About at Home?*

In your practice, you measure production, collections, overhead, and profit. There is a dashboard. There are benchmarks. There is a score.

At home, there is none of that. No dashboard. No score. No clear picture of whether the financial fundamentals are in place or how close you are to your ideal financial condition.

Your household is in some financial condition right now, somewhere on the spectrum between optimal and deficient. The question is: do you know where you stand? And if you don't have a clear picture of what "optimal" looks like, then—how do you know what actions to take to get there?

One of the long-standing gaps in the financial profession is that there has never been a reliable tool to measure whether a healthcare practice owner has the right financial fundamentals in place for their specific situation. Until now.

### *The Financial Prosperity Index®*

The Financial Prosperity Index uses 100 questions to measure the financial fundamentals of a healthcare practice owner's household across nine core areas. The full assessment is available at www.financialprosperityindex.com.

Think of it like a physical exam for your financial life. Just as the human body has multiple systems working together to keep you healthy, your financial life runs on interconnected systems that all affect each other. Ignoring one weakens the whole.

Here are the nine areas the Index evaluates:

- **Financial Planning:** Do you have the right plan, the right financial team, the right infrastructure, and the financial KPIs to guide you toward your goals?

- **Policies and Procedures:** Do you have financial rules governing your household? Have you named an HCFO, or are you still making purely reactive decisions?
- **Business Viability:** Is your practice profitable, sustainable, and transferable? Is it truly supporting your life or just consuming it?
- **Income and Retirement Planning:** Do you know your income targets, your asset requirements, and your timeline for traWWWWWWWWnsitioning out of the practice?
- **Debt and Credit:** Are you managing debt as effectively as you should be?
- **Tax Planning:** Is your team being proactive about minimizing your taxes, or just making sure you are compliant?
- **Estate Planning:** Are your affairs organized and your legacy protected?
- **Asset Protection:** How exposed are you to a lawsuit, a health event, or a major economic disruption?
- **Investments:** Do you know what you own, why you own it, and whether it aligns with your household goals?

There is also a section designed to assess your coachability, your openness to outside advice, and your likelihood of actually following through. That last part matters more than most people want to admit.

***How It Works***

The format is simple. You answer each question Yes, No, or Maybe. The results will be far more useful if you answer based on what is honestly true right now, not how you wish things were or how you hope they will be. As the saying goes, you cannot measure your weight with one foot off the scale.

It is strongly recommended to take the assessment with your spouse. In practice, it rarely creates conflict. What it does create is a real, honest conversation about your finances at a level most couples rarely reach but genuinely need.

Your answers are plotted on a graph that maps the current condition of each of the nine areas and highlights where the gaps are. The result is a score, similar to a credit score, that gives you an immediate and objective picture of your household financial health.

Understanding Your Score

- 700 and above: A solid foundation is in place. You have clarity and control in most areas, though there is always room to strengthen what you have built.
- 400 to 699: The financial basics are lacking in meaningful ways. There are gaps that are increasing your risk exposure and limiting

your progress. These are fixable, but they require attention.

- Below 400: The household is under real financial duress. The basics are largely absent and the risk of asset loss is significant. This is the most urgent category, and also the one where improvement creates the most immediate impact.

There is no judgment attached to any score. This is not about where you are. It is about where you go next.

Avoiding the diagnosis does not improve the condition.

Some people are afraid to take the assessment because they fear what they will find. Others skip it out of overconfidence, convinced they are doing just fine while significant unseen risks are quietly building. Both responses are understandable. Neither one is useful.

You have patients who avoid annual checkups for these exact same reasons. You know how that story usually ends.

***What Happens After You Complete the Assessment***

Once you finish the questionnaire, here is what you will have:

- Your score across all nine financial areas
- A clear view of your strengths and where the gaps are
- Reduced uncertainty about your actual financial condition
- Specific guidance on what steps to take next

Completing the assessment and reviewing your score does not obligate you to work with Econologics Financial Advisors. But it will give you something far more valuable than a sales pitch: an honest, objective picture of where your household stands today.

What will truly change your condition is picking up your feet and doing the work one step at a time. The Econologics® Roadmap is designed to give you the exact tools and strategies to move you toward the top of the graph.

The advisors at EFA work alongside you through the entire financial planning process to make sure the recommendations get implemented and the results actually show up. The program works when it is applied. It does not work when it is set aside.

What Is a Power Move?

A power move is a decisive action, taken at the right time, that permanently changes your trajectory. You have made power moves before. Buying your practice was one. Hiring your first associate was one. Deciding to expand was one.

This is the financial version of that move.

Here is what a power move looks like:

- ✓ Set aside the time
- ✓ Take the assessment at www.financialprosperityindex.com

- ✓ Answer every question with complete honesty
- ✓ Schedule your session to review the results with the EFA team

You can no longer afford to be reactive in your personal finances, always guessing about what might happen next. You have spent years building a practice that runs with intention and structure. Your household deserves the same.

You built a successful practice. Now it is time to build a successful life.

Make the power move. Your household deserves it!

Take the Financial Prosperity Index Assessment

# ABOUT THE AUTHOR

Eric S. Miller
Financial Planning Expert for Healthcare Practice Owners
*Specializing in the fields of Veterinary, Optometry, Physical Therapy, etc.*

Eric Miller is a Registered Financial Consultant (RFC®), licensed insurance professional, and co-owner of Econologics Financial Advisors, LLC a Registered Investment Advisory firm and national insurance agency where he serves as Principal and Chief Financial Advisor.

With more than 20 years of experience, Eric has worked with over 500 healthcare practice owners across the country, helping them navigate the financial realities of building, growing, and ultimately exiting their businesses. His work focuses on bringing structure, clarity, and control to both the practice and the household—guiding clients through every stage of ownership.

Under Eric's leadership, Econologics Financial Advisors was named to the Inc. 5000 list of fastest-growing companies in the United States in both 2019 and 2020—a reflection of the firm's impact and growth nationwide.

Eric and his team have been involved in more than 40 practice transitions, representing over $230 million in total value. In addition to comprehensive financial planning, their work spans debt and credit management, asset protection, tax strategy, and exit planning. The firm also manages or oversees nearly $200 million in client assets.

Beyond his advisory work, Eric is a prolific educator, best-selling author, and speaker. He is the author of *The Financial Beast®: How to Harness the Power of Your Practice to Build Personal Wealth and Go Out at the Top of Your Game* and the host of the popular *Financial Beast Podcast* for practice owners. Eric has also authored numerous articles, recorded podcasts and videos, and spoken at hundreds of live and virtual events nationwide. His content is focused on helping practice owners avoid common financial mistakes and implement strategies that lead to long-term financial control and independence.

This book reflects Eric's core philosophy: when the household is treated as the primary financial entity—and the practice is structured to serve it—true financial clarity, control, and long-term success become possible.

# Econologics Financial Advisors

Econologics Financial Advisors, LLC is a Registered Investment Advisory firm and national insurance agency that works with healthcare practice owners and associates across the United States. The firm focuses on helping clients bring structure and clarity to their financial lives by integrating business and household finances into one coordinated system.

Through its planning process and ongoing advisory support, Econologics helps practice owners make more informed decisions as they build, grow, and eventually transition their businesses.

Econologics Financial Advisors has worked with hundreds of clients nationwide and has been involved in numerous successful practice transitions. The firm's approach is grounded in a simple idea: when the practice is structured to support the household, financial progress becomes more organized, intentional, and sustainable.

Explore more resources and tools for practice owners:

Website: www.EconologicsFinancialAdvisors.com

Phone: (727) 588-1540

Made in the USA
Coppell, TX
04 August 2026

85681418R00066